YOUR SACRED STORY

How Relationships, Sexuality and Spirituality Shape Us

Robert E. Lauder

Resurrection Press
Mineola • New York

Dedicated with love to Emily, Maura, Liam, Katherine,
Regina and Matthew,
six gifts from God, and to Fran Fico whose cheerful outgoing
personality is a sign of God's presence.

Grateful acknowledgement is made to The Long Island Catholic *for material which previously appeared in its pages.*

Excerpts from "Faithful Love" and "Instruments of God" from *May I Have This Dance* by Joyce Rupp, copyright 1992 by Ave Maria, Notre Dame, IN 46556. Used with permission of the publisher.

First published in 1998 by Resurrection Press, Ltd.
P.O. Box 248, Williston Park, NY 11596

ISBN 1-878718-42-8
Library of Congress Catalog Card Number 98-66236

Cover design by John Murello.

Printed in the United States of America.

Contents

Above all, trust in the slow work of God.
We are, quite naturally,
  impatient in everything
  to reach the end without delay.

We should like to skip
  the intermediate stages;
we are impatient of being on the way
  to something unknown,
  something new.
And yet, it is the law of all progress
  that it is made by passing through
  some stages of instability...
  and that may take a very long time.

—PIERRE TEILHARD DE CHARDIN

Foreword

FLIP OPEN ANY ONE of the Gospels and peruse with a weather eye cocked for the relationships you find there— the relationship between Mary and the angel who brings her such startling news; the relationship between Joseph and Mary; the relationship between Jesus and John the Baptizer; the relationships between Jesus and his disciples, Jesus and the Pharisees, Jesus and Nicodemus, Jesus and the rich young man, the widowed mother whose son has died, Martha and Mary, between Jesus and his Father, and on and on... Observe these relationships, and you may be surprised and delighted at what you find in the Gospels that you never found before.

Thus do the Gospels teach us the true meaning of spirituality, that it is not a focus on Someplace Else, pie in the sky, bye and bye, when you die. The Gospels teach us that spirituality is first of all about relationships, here and now —between God and us, between us and other people, and between us and the earth our home. Our spirituality, as Father Lauder so rightly says, is about how we *think* and *act* in these relationships. An authentic Christian spirituality is, in other words, never an abstraction or a theory. An authentic Christian spirituality is *life*. Here and now.

Finally, the most overlooked dimension of the Gospels is the *sexuality* of the people who populate the Gospels. True, we hear more than we once did about *feminine* presence in the Gospels, and this is good. Some highly significant characters in the Gospels are women, starting with, but not limited to, Mary the mother of Jesus. What can women and men learn from the feminine presence in the

Gospels? What can we learn from the woman who gives her last few coins, the women who stand at the foot of the cross, the women who are the first witnesses to the Resurrection? Given such a feminine witness, can we ever downplay the value of feminine presence in the Church?

Rarely taken into account, however, is *masculine* presence in the Gospels. Ideologically incorrect as it may be to point this out in a feminist era, the Gospels were written and edited by men, Jesus is a man, the twelve apostles are men, and many of the characters in the Gospel stories are men. What can men and women learn from this? Can we, for example, ever accept the popular cultural prejudice which infers that men who are religious somehow compromise their masculinity?

Father Robert E. Lauder is a professor of philosophy at a Catholic university, yet his writing is anything but "ivory tower." He speaks of God and people as one who lives in the knockabout world, the world of glorious joy and tremendous anguish, and he speaks in the spirit of the Gospel. Therefore, his words carry good news, indeed. He reminds us that we tell an unmatchable story by living our lives, by the relationships that fill our lives, by the spirituality that guides and inspires us, and by being the feminine and masculine friends God created us to be with one another.

Whisper a simple prayer asking the Holy Spirit to touch your heart through the words you are about to read. For the Holy Spirit is in these words, waiting to bubble up in the center of your being and increase in you the gift of eternal life...here and now.

—MITCH FINLEY

Introduction

SOMETHING IS HAPPENING to large numbers of people. It seems as though more and more people are struggling to make sense of their lives, "to get their act together," to find meaning or meanings that can tie together the various seemingly unrelated strands of their life into a coherent pattern that provides fulfillment and happiness. That people are doing this is cause for me as a priest and a professor of philosophy to rejoice. The capacity to reflect on the meaning of our lives is one of the great gifts that God has given us. We are not robots moving through the world without insight or intuition nor are we animals instinctively responding to stimuli. We are persons, the most gifted creatures on God's earth.

In trying to make sense of my own life I have found the notion of spirituality and the metaphor of story especially illuminating. These reflections on spirituality and story are offered in the hope that readers might be helped in shaping their own lives into a coherent pattern. I am writing this book about story to encourage you to become aware of God's presence in your life, and of how your life has been and is surrounded by God's love.

Instruments of God

...my often-empty life
rests in the hand of God;
like the hollowed flute,
it yearns for the melody
which only breath can give.

the small, wooden flute and I,
we need the one who breathes,
we await one who makes melody.

and the one whose touch creates,
awaits our empty, ordinary forms,
so that the song-starved world
may be fed with golden melodies.

—JOYCE RUPP

Chapter I

HOW GOD AND OTHERS SHAPE OUR STORY

EVERYONE LOVES a story. Whether we hear them, watch them on a television screen, on a stage or in a movie theater, stories have a special fascination. If a preacher or teacher wants rapt attention, he or she tells a story. There seems to be a profound need in us to which stories speak. Jewish writer Elie Wiesel claims that God created human beings because God loves stories.

Though we may love stories, we may not be aware how influential stories are in forming and shaping us. In his *What Is God? How to Think about the Divine* (Paulist Press, New York, 1986) theologian John Haught emphasizes the influence of story in our formation:

"The identity of all of us is established by our interaction with the narrative context of our existences. Our sense of meaning of our lives, if we are fortunate enough to be conscious of living meaningfully, is a gift of the narrative nest in which we dwell. The meaning of our lives is determined by the way in which each of us participates in an ongoing story. And where people today speak of their experience of meaninglessness, isolation, alienation, rootlessness, etc., such experiences can almost invariably be traced to an inability to find some meaningful story in which to situate our lives." (p. 74)

Each of us is a product of various stories which make us who we are. I am influenced by the story of Western civilization, by the story of the United States, by the New York story, by the story of my parents, by the story of my sister. Growing up I was enormously influenced by the story of the family that lived next door to my family. Looking over my life I realize that I have been profoundly influenced by the stories of two families with whom I have spent a great deal of time, and by the story of one of my closest friends with whom I studied for the priesthood. He and I shared wonderful dreams about how we were going to transform the Church and in the process transform the world. My life interacts with the stories of my students at St. John's University and with the professors and university staff with whom I work. Who I am is connected to the story of the Pope and my bishop and related to the stories of all to whom I try to minister as a priest. Years ago in his *Ascent of the Mountain, Flight of the Dove: An Invitation to Religious Studies* (Harper & Row, New York, 1971) Michael Novak succinctly articulated the nature of story:

> "What is a story? A story is a narrative that links sequences. A story is a structure for time. A story links actions over time. The more integrated a life, the more all things in it work toward a single (perhaps comprehensive) direction. The richer a life, the more subplots the story encompasses. Interesting people are full of contradictions. Strong drives of various sorts compete in them. They are motivated simultaneously by ambition and gentleness, hostility and humble charity, weakness and strength. To bring integration out of wildly disparate tendencies is the mark of a great soul..." (p.49)

We Write Our Story

In a sense I am my story. Our personal identity is formed, shaped and created by the story that we write through our choices and especially through the commitments we make. You are what you do. Your actions flow from your self-identity and then contribute to that identity in your journey through life.

As I reflect on all the stories that have influenced me, I am aware of a handful of people who have had a profound effect on me. One was a young man who I met in my first year of college. Eight years my senior, he was the first person I had ever met whom I could identify as a Catholic intellectual—someone who intelligently related his Catholic faith to politics, current events and contemporary thought. He introduced me to the prestigious Catholic magazine, *Commonweal,* which I had never heard of. I subscribed to it because I wanted to be able to relate the Catholic faith to current events the way my friend did. I wanted to think as I thought a Catholic should think. Even now, more than forty years later, I can recall my excitement when my first issue of *Commonweal* arrived.

The more I think about the interaction of my story with the stories of others, the more I become aware of the gift dimension of my life. I suspect that most people believe that their parents and family are special people. Mine were. If my sister was not a saint, then I guess I never met a saint. A friend of mine claims that all parents should go straight to heaven because of the sacrifices they make for their children. It would be silly for me to try to list the blessings I received from my parents. Where would I begin? Where would I end? I just know that whatever is

good in me came through them. They were two great
human beings.

There probably is no reality that influences our stories
more than our religion does. Our religion is radical. It
drives us and colors what we do and who we are. Michael
Novak said it well:

> "Religion is the acting out of a vision of personal identi-
> ty and human community. Religion is constituted by the
> most ultimate, least easily surrendered, most comprehen-
> sive choices a person or society acts out ... Religion is a way
> of perceiving oneself, others, the world; a way of acting."
> (*Ascent of the Mountain*, p. 27)

When I think of my religion, I feel especially gifted.
What did I do to deserve being a Catholic? My story is
tied to the story of the Jewish people. Abraham is my
father in faith. My story is especially tied to the story of
Jesus. Without Jesus' birth, life, death and resurrection I
would not have a story. Without Jesus there is no pattern
or narrative to human life. Without the story of Jesus,
human persons are merely the chance product of evolu-
tion. Without the story of Jesus, human life is not going
anywhere. Without the story of Jesus, I am adrift in space,
a mistake with no meaningful past and no hope-filled
future.

God's Loving Presence

As we reflect on our story and look for a meaningful pattern, we remind ourselves that we are not alone, that
God's loving presence pervades our experience. The hand
of God is present throughout our lives. With the light of
our faith we can try to discern God's loving presence in

our lives.

One of the mistakes that we make when we think of God's presence in our lives is that we think of God as a physical presence, as a physical cause that "makes" things happen. It seems as though our minds go from one extreme to the other: we either think of God present in our lives as a physical cause "making" or "forcing" things to happen or we think of God as a distant spectator not at all involved in our lives. I believe that the truth is that God is completely involved in our lives but not as a physical cause. Rather God is completely involved in our lives as a loving presence. God does not "make" things happen or "force" things to happen but through the loving presence of God we are invited to be caring, compassionate people. We can reject God's loving presence if we choose. God will not force us to accept His self-gift. But if we do freely accept God's self-gift, then we are saved or redeemed.

God's loving presence is a constant in our lives. While we are in charge of our lives and must take responsibility for what we do, we are not writing our stories alone. We are writing them in response to the loving presence of God. We are not alone in the universe; we have not been abandoned; we are not isolated. We are loved beyond our capacity to imagine. No matter how much we think about God's love for us we will never be able to imagine it or even to understand it. God's love goes beyond our wildest imaginings and dreams and it is that love that we are called to respond to in our lives. That love can color our entire lives if we allow it to transform us. That love calls us to relate to other persons with love and concern.

Some believers seem to spot God's involvement in their lives easily. They claim that God sent people into their lives, that God caused events to occur in their lives, that God moved them to make particular decisions. I tend to be skeptical with what I perceive as a too easy identification of God's causality with all sorts of happenings. I am not denying God's loving presence in our lives; I am just being a little cautious about identifying God as intervening in our lives in some particular or specific way.

I cannot deny that God occasionally may cause some event to happen in a person's life but I think that God's presence is more wonderful than the occasional intervention. If we look at our entire lives, if we try to articulate the goodness that we experience in our lives, we may get a better sense of God's constant presence. It's not the special intervention that is so marvelous even if that intervention is a miracle. That God has surrounded us with His love is what is important. The story of every human life is a story of love—God's love and our response to or rejection of that love.

Self, Others, Community

The balance between being an individual and being a member of a community is very difficult to achieve and maintain. If we become lost in a group, if we allow others to do our thinking for us, then we just will not grow as human persons. However if we try to go it alone, we inevitably miss all sorts of opportunities for personal growth. I have come to believe that a person completely alone is a contradiction, a square circle. We are made by God for others. The simplest way of articulating this truth is, "I cannot be I on the deepest level of my self without you; you cannot be you on the deepest level of your self without me."

I had a rather humorous experience that illustrates the difficulties that can arise in community but also the unexpected joys that community can provide. I spent my summer vacation with eleven children. One was 14 years of age, three were 12 and the others ranged from two years of age to eight. Making a kind of miniature football team, all were children of friends. I found out I was neither quarterback nor captain of the team. The vacation was a unique experience.

When we arrived at the site, a lovely peaceful spot near water, the parents of some of the children and I started unloading our cars. Two of the parents saw me carrying some books into the house. The wife smilingly commented while her husband laughed out loud, "You brought books!" That I would bring books on a vacation did not seem amusing to me. I pictured myself sitting on the porch or near the water or in my room reading peacefully. It never happened.

Here is the basic pattern of each day:

I, along with one or two parents, lug out into the sun a gigantic tub of toys that would make anyone suspect that F.A.O. Schwartz had been raided. Along with the toys we carried out swimmies, beach shoes, tennis balls, a football, beach balls, a frisbee, and assorted gardening tools such as rakes, spades and pails that looked as though they might have been left over from the filming of *Tobacco Road*. Also we dragged along with us some beach blankets, beach towels and beach chairs. Believe me the journey from indoors to outdoors bore some resemblance to the Exodus.

After all the paraphernalia were put out on the beach, things were carefully sorted and the beach blankets were gently laid out completely free from sand. They stayed that way for almost a minute before the two-year-old marched across them carrying on his feet what looked like a considerable portion of the Sahara. Still I felt a sense of relief and joyful expectation as I propped myself up in one of the beach chairs ready to oversee the children, happily holding in my hand one of the books that I had brought.

The children seemed to take my plans to read as some kind of challenge. No sooner did I get myself creamed from head to toe with suntan lotion, put on my hat and sun glasses, than one of the children said, "Let's go swimming!" Since it had taken some time to get settled, this idea did not appeal to me; but I was definitely in the minority. With several children racing ahead of me I picked up a beach chair, hopefully hugged my book and walked down to the water's edge, planted my possessions and followed the screaming children into the water. It took me a moment or two to get into the water and another moment to walk further in so that the water was up to my waist. I stood there for a second and then dove into what seemed icy water. As I came up from the water I noticed that I was now soaking wet, a little cold and completely alone. As I looked behind me I saw the children racing back up to the blanket because they had decided that they preferred playing up near the blanket rather than staying in the water. I trudged behind them, trying not to get my book wet.

At one point in the vacation we were a little pressed for space. I was not concerned because I had claimed possession of a really good bed in a room by myself. One evening as I lay down completely exhausted, a six-year-old little girl climbed in next to me and cuddled her face in my neck so that her mouth was very close to my ear. How lovely I thought. How affectionate she is. As she snuggled to make herself comfortable she whispered in my ear, "The last time I slept with my Daddy I throwed up on him." I tried to keep calm. I said, "Oh, that was O.K." She said, "No, it went all over his hair." Refusing to overreact, I said, "I am sure he didn't mind." She said, "Yes, he did. He had to wash his hair." I was afraid to ask her how her stomach felt at that moment.

Actually my bed was not as comfortable as I thought it would be. Some of the children periodically walked across it, their little toes sprinkling sand on my sheets. Have you ever slept in sandy sheets? By the end of the vacation my admiration for members of the Foreign Legion had grown considerably.

Prior to Mass one day I was assigning the scripture readings to some of the parents when one five-year-old looked me in the eyes and said, "I think it would be good if we let the children read instead of just choosing your friends."

It was quite a vacation. Can you believe it? I had a fabulous time.

In his *The Christian Vision of Humanity: Basic Christian Anthropology* (Liturgical Press, Collegeville, Minnesota, 1991), Father John R. Sachs, S.J. says some important things about the individual and community. Stressing that community is essential for personal growth Father Sachs writes:

> "Such community can only come about when human persons relate to each other personally, and that means in relationships based upon equality, mutuality and affection...But real community is not just the sharing of a common trait, interest or experience. It is the desire to share one's own self in love. It is based on the positive bonding of mutual affection. This is the difference between society and true community.

"For community to be full, it must be inclusive. It must continue and develop the self-transcendence and other-relatedness that characterizes each one of us as a human being. The end toward which such growth tends is a community without limit in which all persons are free to become fully active in love." (p. 38)

There is much to reflect on in Father Sachs' depiction of a real community. The first important point is that just because we occupy the same space with other people—at a job or in a house or in a school—does not mean that we are in a community with them. Genuine community demands much more than mere physical presence. If a relationship is going to have any depth, the minimum required is that the equality of persons be recognized and that any bigotry or prejudice be absent. But that is just the minimum.

What is required in a real community is a bonding of love. It is this bonding in real love that makes a family a tremendously creative force in the life of any individual; it is the absence of love in a family that can make a family an incredibly destructive force. What influences us, for better or for worse, more than our families? How many marvelous gifts in a person's personality or life can be traced back to an individual's family? How many disappointments, unfulfilled dreams and lifelong problems can be traced back to an individual's family? While we cannot attribute who we are to anyone other than ourselves, it is true that our families have played a crucial role in our lives.

In mentioning a person's self-transcendence and other-relatedness, Father Sachs touches on the deepest dimension of personal existence. To be self-transcendent is to be never finished, open to the future, self-creative. To be self-transcendent is to be a mystery even to yourself. To be self-transcendent is to be responsible for your self. There are many directions that a person can take in his or her life. Some directions lead to personal growth; some directions lead to self-destruction.

A key to understanding the direction we should take in our lives is to realize that we are other-directed. We are directed toward other human persons, and we are directed toward God. The easiest and most direct way to self-destruct is to be selfish and self-centered. Through selfishness and self-centeredness we shrink ourselves as persons. Through self-sacrifice and love we expand and deepen the personal dimension of our existence. Each of our lives is unique, but there are some basic truths which are at the core of every one of us. One of these truths is that to be a person is to be called to love. Responding to that call in a community is one of the marvelous ways that we grow as persons. Everyone writes his or her own story through his or her free choices. As we make our choices we are creating ourselves and writing our stories.

An Overarching Story

I have come to realize the importance of believing that there is an overarching story within which each of our individual stories takes place. This overarching story is always more than we can ever articulate clearly. The overarching story involves the mystery of God's presence within our story.

Let's consider a young woman, who is intensely interested in track. Imagine that this young lady has made all sorts of sacrifices in order to participate in the Olympics.

As the date for the Olympics draws near she breaks her leg in a fall and it is clear that she will not be able to compete in the Olympics. Her initial reaction is that participating in the Olympics was her lifelong dream and that her life is now over. As she recovers she can see that there are many important things in her life, some even more important than participating in the Olympics. Besides the story of her life geared toward the Olympics there is a deeper story, an overarching story that provides sufficient meaning for her to carry on her life. She discovers that there is more to her life than the Olympics.

Religious faith tells us that there is an overarching story that encompasses our individual stories. That overarching story gives each person's story ultimate meaning. Without the overarching story of God's ongoing love affair with the human race we would have to conclude that human existence is absurd, that it is a futile effort with no real purpose to it. John Haught makes this point clearly:

> "The 'death of God' does seem to entail the collapse of narrative as the matrix for our lives. The inability to think about God in any meaningful sense undermines the idea of there being any overarching meaning to history or to the universe as such. And when the cosmos and history are themselves perceived as purposeless, then the individual's life-story (if one can call it a story at all) will be seen as nothing more than a disjointed series of moments played out on a stage that is deaf to any cry for meaning. Without the support of a transcendent ground, therefore, life-inspiring narrative can be no more than a chimera. Once people begin to suspect that there is no such ground, the cosmic and historic narratives that attempt to locate their lives in the total scheme of things will also lose their

power." (*What Is God?*, p. 76)

But because of God's involvement with our stories, not only is human life not absurd but it has a meaning that is so magnificent that it is mystery, so marvelous that it transcends our capacity to comprehend it completely, so profound that the most brilliant human mind cannot understand it totally. Human life is an exciting drama precisely because it is a potential love affair with the Divine. The stakes in any human story are very high, almost incredibly high. What is at stake is eternity.

As a Catholic Christian I believe that the story of Jesus is in a special way the story of God's relationship with us. In Jesus we discover what God has done for us, is doing and will do. Through Jesus Christ we discover that our story has been tied to God's story and that our story will stretch into eternity. Through Jesus' Resurrection we discover that the love story between God and us will never end.

Story and Imagination

In reflecting on my story while trying to write this book, I have come to appreciate the role that imagination plays in everyone's life. Recently I had to do four television shows, and on each show I was going to interview two people. Of the eight people whom I invited to appear with me, five were hesitant to participate because they felt that they did not know enough about the topic. I had chosen the eight people very carefully, so I was certain that they would do well in the television discussions. What was it that was discouraging the five from accepting my invitation? It was their imaginations. They could not imagine themselves being at ease on television, intelligently discussing the topic I had chosen. In fact their imaginations were telling them that they would make fools of themselves. In order to persuade them to participate I had to imagine with them just how the shows would go and imagine with them the contributions they would be able to make. Finally they did agree to do the shows, and each of the guests was marvelous. In fact, they were better than I imagined they would be.

This experience made me realize just how much our imaging of ourselves can limit us. Our imaginations can give us very negative and false pictures of ourselves. Just as our imaginations can lead us more deeply into the mystery of human living, they can also prevent us or hinder us from growing.

One reason why I created a Catholic novel course is that I became aware of the enormous power of images. Contemporary advertising powerfully and persuasively presents the gospel of consumerism. Reading Catholic novels is one antidote. I believe that by opening ourselves to the images in a Catholic novel we will not only be educated by great literature but we may be challenged by faith images. By reading them we are feeding our imaginations in a unique way. Catholic novels of Graham Greene, Evelyn Waugh, Francois Mauriac, George Bernanos, Walker Percy, Jon Hassler, Shusaku Endo, Morris West are hidden treasures. The dramatization of Catholic faith in a well written novel can have a positive influence on both our consciousness and our conscience.

Catholic novels can both challenge and enlighten us about God. We may alter our image of God when a Catholic novel dramatizes that God is the "Hound of Heaven" relentlessly pursuing us, passionately in love with us, eager to shower many blessings upon us. Some great Catholic novels highlight that we don't need to win or earn God's love but rather that God is an eager Lover who desires a love relationship with us. Catholic novels can illuminate in our lives the presence of God who is helping us write our stories.

Questions

1. How would you describe your story?

2. What stories have contributed to your story?

3. Where do you think of God as most present in your experience?

4. Is community important in your life?

5. To what communities do you belong? Which have influenced or are influencing you the most?

6. Does your imagination help your spirituality? How?

Batter my heart, three-personed God; for you
As yet but knock, breathe, shine, and seek to mend.
That I may rise, and stand, o'erthrow me, and bend
Your force, to break, blow, burn, and make me new.

...Take me to you, imprison me, for I
Except you enthrall me, never shall be free,
Nor ever chaste, except you ravish me.

—JOHN DONNE

Chapter II

HOW OUR SPIRITUALITY AND SEXUALITY MOLD OUR STORY

BY SPIRITUALITY I mean the way that a person conceives of self, neighbor and God and the living out of those conceptions. A spirituality is not merely a way of thinking but a way of thinking and acting. An individual might describe his or her spirituality in one way but actually live a completely different spirituality from the one described. Probably the best way to identify a spirituality is to examine how we live. A style of living should reveal a person's real spirituality more accurately than the words or concepts that a person might use to describe it. In reflecting on our spiritualities we need to examine not only how we think about God, self, and neighbor but how we translate those ideas into our prayer life and into our daily living. So spirituality is composed of understanding and also on how that understanding is or is not incorporated into a person's life. Stories shape spiritualities and spiritualities write stories.

There was a time in my life when my spirituality was very much centered around my own efforts at growing closer to God. Of course we have to make efforts to grow spiritually but looking back on my efforts I have come to see that an enormous amount of neurotic guilt influenced my actions. I suspect that much of my spiritual effort had a compulsive component to it. More activity on my part always seemed better than less activity and so the multiplication of prayers and devotions were an important part of my spirituality. There was a kind of perfectionism that permeated my view of the spiritual life and my attempts at growing in grace. Though I would never have said that we save ourselves, that may have been what I at least implicitly thought and the way I lived. Growth in the spiritual life depended a great deal on my efforts. Somewhere along the way my attitude changed. This was a long process but I believe it was a change for the better. I don't think that I have slipped into the heresy of quietism, the heresy of thinking that God will save me without any action on my part, but there definitely has been a shift of emphasis in what I think about God and my relationship with the Divine.

I now think of the spiritual life as primarily listening to God and responding to what God says to me. I try to put the emphasis on God rather than Lauder. Everything in the spiritual life starts with God. We do not initiate, we do not start the relationship, we do not get God's attention so that God will shower blessings and graces on us. The initiative begins with God. Without His initiative nothing can happen that will benefit us. There is no picking ourselves up by our bootstraps. There are no self-made Christians. The Kingdom of God comes from above and our membership in it is a gift from God. Our story is begun by God and God's loving presence permeates the drama of our lives.

Reflecting on our spirituality is one way of reflecting on the story of our lives, the story that we are writing with God. By focusing on our spirituality we are focusing our attention on what we think is essential to our lives of faith.

Unfortunately we can get stuck in a spirituality that does not call us to growth, a spirituality that does not call us into a deeper understanding of ourselves, does not help us to be more sensitive to our neighbors and does not move us to fall more deeply in love with God. I think of St. Paul's words:

"When I was a child, I spoke as a child, I felt as a child, I thought as a child. Now that I have become a man, I have put away the things of a child." (1 Cor 13:11)

We grow physically, emotionally and psychologically. We ought to grow spiritually. If my understanding of myself in relation to God and others is still what it was when I was seven years old then something is wrong. If my images of God are the same as when I was a child then something is wrong. We are creatures of habit. It is so easy for us to conduct our lives in the mode and manner of "business as usual." We do not want that to happen in relation to God.

Thinking about my own spirituality I have come to see that what has changed dramatically in my own life is the realization that I do not have to win, earn or merit God's love. My own education and training put such an emphasis on the sinfulness of the human person and the need to win God's affection that it took me a long time to realize that *God does not love us because we are lovable but rather that we are lovable because God loves us.* God's love is creative and Divine love makes us who we are. In relation to us God is all love. God never withdraws that love.

I can vividly recall making a day of prayer and the nun who was giving it said, "God will never love you more than he does at this moment." My initial reaction to that statement was discomfort. I was trained to think that I had to earn God's love so the truth that God loved me totally and without reservation, was difficult for me to accept. I believe that it is difficult for many people to accept this incredible truth.

"Accepting acceptance" is one way of articulating what our basic attitude toward God should be. We should accept that God has accepted us with no strings attached, with no conditions that need to be fulfilled by us. God just loves us unconditionally and constantly. When we retire at night God is loving us, while we are sleeping God is loving us, when we wake up in the morning God is loving us. Perhaps the greatest act of faith that we need to make is believing that God is passionately in love with us. Perhaps the greatest act of faith that I have to make is not that God is in love with the human race, not that God loves all people but that God loves me.

Shame, the feeling that there is something about us that is unacceptable to us and to others, can be fostered by people that make extreme demands of us, demands that we cannot fulfill. We can feel shame because we fail to live up to the expectations that come from our family or from some academic, emotional or psychological standards that are imposed on us.

There are no standards or requirements imposed on us by God in order for God to love us. God just loves us. The good news that Jesus brought is about the incomprehensible love that God has for each of us. No image we have of God's love for us is ever going to be sufficient or adequate because God will always love us more than we can imagine. Jesus' crucifixion is the strongest image we have.

In his *Mystery and Promise: A Theology of Revelation* (Liturgical Press, Collegeville, Minnesota, 1993), John Haught writes beautifully of God's loving identification with our shame in the crucified Jesus:

> "In Jesus' teaching about God, our childish projection of a deity who scrutinizes our performance and keeps a record of it as a basis for accepting or rejecting us is shattered. And in Christian faith's never fully cherished identification of God with the crucified Christ, the projection is radically dismantled. Death by crucifixion was quite probably the most shameful situation imaginable for an individual at the time of Jesus...The corresponding image of God as one who embraces this depth of human shame as an aspect of the divine life amounts to nothing less than a metaphysical abolition of all the alternative ideas of God....By identifying with the outcast Jesus, the man slain through the most shameful form of execution, God is disclosed as one who includes all that we normally exclude. And this means not only others that we may have rejected. It also includes our own weakness and shame." (p.194)

I like very much Haught's expression "never fully cherished identification of God with the crucified Christ." Certainly I have never fully cherished that identification and I know that other Christians haven't. I have heard Christians speak of the crucified Christ as though he did not really suffer and die. Our Christian faith is that Jesus is really human as well as being divine. This means that he really suffered and it also means that God experiences the most shameful death. More basic than any other standard that we impose on ourselves or that others impose on us is the profound truth that God places no standard or conditions on us in order for God to love us. If that love is not enough for us to be a trusting, hope-filled people then nothing is.

A Christian Sexuality

There is a belief among many that if a storyteller wants to be commercially successful he or she must lace the story with sex. Required in a best selling novel are some steamy love scenes or in a successful film some bedroom scenes, so the conventional wisdom says. Of course beyond the capacity of such scenes to titillate readers or audiences there is the undeniable power of sex and the absolutely indispensable role that sex plays in the life of every person. Sex plays an indispensable role in the life of the married person, in the life of the single person and in the life of the celibate. To be a human person is to be a sexual person. If the story of our lives is going to be as beautiful as God desires, it is crucial that we try to integrate our sexuality into our personalities. A glance at our society confirms that this is not an easy task.

I am amazed as I continue to discover elements of Jansenism and Puritanism in my outlook on sexuality. For much of my life I associated sex primarily with sin. Many "good" Catholics seem to have the same problem. Strange that we do not do this with any other of our appetites or desires. We don't think of thirst or hunger or the desire for beauty or the desire for truth as primarily connected with sin. My thinking stems from an emphasis in my seminary training on the danger of sexual sin. Either it was the training or it was my personality but I don't recall any attempt at helping us integrate our sexuality into our personalities so that we might be closer to God, more capable of loving and more effective servants of God.

It seems humorous now to recall that one of the priests who was instructing us said, "After you are ordained, never call a woman by her first name!" Could such a statement come out of a Christian view of sexuality? I think that today some marvelous things are being written about a Christian outlook on sexuality and I suspect that on every level of Catholic education a more balanced approach is being taken toward sexuality. Our sexuality is a marvelous gift from God and we want to integrate it into our personalities so that we can relate more lovingly to one another.

Unfortunately Christians can feel shame about one of the most marvelous gifts God has bestowed on people— their sexuality. In his book *Mystery and Promise: A Theology of Revelation* John Haught writes with insight about shame:

> "Shame is the feeling that takes over us when we begin to become aware of an aspect of our being that seems unacceptable both to us and to those in our social environment. Shame is a universal human phenomenon, and in a certain sense it is a necessary response to the facts of social existence...But shame may also lead us into self-deception. It may push completely out of consciousness that which we take to be unacceptable in ourselves. Thus we may completely forget essential chapters of our own life stories and repress obvious facets of our personalities for the sake of wanting to fit into some social or even religious habitat. Shame holds us back therefore from full self-knowledge, freedom, and the fulfillment of our personal lives." (p.186)

Freud was wrong about God but I think he had marvelous insights into the mystery of sexuality and the powerful influence, for better or worse, that a person's sexual nature can have in his or her life. Allowing the Christian view of sex to enter deeply into our consciousness and to integrate it into our personalities is a lifelong task.

Sexuality, Chastity and Friendship

Even a cursory glance at contemporary American society would reveal what a powerful force sex can be and how disordered and unruly a person's sexuality can become. The breakup of marriages, the difficulty that many single people have about making a life commitment in marriage, the almost complete ignorance of the value of celibacy, the lack of fidelity in marriage relationships, problems of sexual harassment and sexual abuse and the apparent ubiquity of pornography—even reaching into the world of children—point to the problem that sex has become in our society. The Christian is trying to walk a line between a Jansenism and Puritanism that does not appreciate God's gift of sexuality and a kind of paganism that seems to be promoted in much of the media. Human experience shows that the line is not easily walked. Unfortunately, even among Christians who take their faith very seriously, tinges of Jansenism and Puritanism can be found, attitudes that neglect the beauty of sexuality and almost suggest that being sexual is at best a necessary evil.

I have come to believe that the first step toward living chastely is to see sex as one of God's great gifts to the human race. Any repression of our sexuality works against Christian chastity and ultimately against Christian charity. In his excellent *By Way of the Heart: Toward a*

Holistic Christian Spirituality (Paulist Press, New York, 1989) Wilkie Au writes with great insight about repression.

> "Some people so fear their sexual feelings that they endeavor to cap them through denial. For them, erotic feelings are like potential terrorists threatening to hijack the ship of self and steer it uncontrollably into dangerous waters. Consciously or unconsciously, they feel that the best way to avoid this danger is to pretend that these potentially disruptive forces are not present. When this denial is done unconsciously, it is called repression. Through the defense mechanism of repression, individuals block from their consciousness unwanted feelings and impulses. But both denial and repression are ineffective ways of coping with sexual feelings because they exclude awareness." (p.145)

Au's description fits the way I dealt with my sexuality for a large portion of my life. How that happened I do not know but I somehow came to equate repression with virtue and I paid for that error in many ways. It is impossible to even approach emotional balance unless sexuality is integrated in a healthy way into our personalities. Repression is basically a lie and it prevents us from dealing intelligently with our sexuality. To deny our sexuality can hurt us psychologically. Such a denial can foster rigid and angry personalities. The sad truth is that such a denial does not foster Christian chastity. Sexuality has within it a power that can help us relate to others warmly and with affection. To deny that power and to try to live as though it did not exist is to deny what it means to be human.

Rather than repression, Christians and others should engage in what has come to be called suppression. This is the *conscious* control of our sexual appetite and drives for the sake of some clearly chosen goals and values. Everyone should do this: married people, single people and celibate people. A therapist friend of mine describes the contemporary abuse of sex in our society as the loss of the superego. In Freud's analysis of sexuality he claimed that every person had a superego and by that he meant a blind censor which kept the sexual and aggressive drives under control. People's superegos according to Freud were greatly influenced by their parents but also by the societies in which they lived. Freud claimed that without the superego human society would be chaos with people acting out their every desire. For example without the superego men would go about raping women. Even without buying into Freud's entire theory of sexuality we can see signs that there is little restraint in our society concerning sexuality. One statistic I heard recently claimed that in this country a woman is raped every fifteen seconds.

While repression is extremely unhealthy, suppression can be a marvelous tool in channeling the power within our sexuality. Suppression can help us be more affectionate, more sensitive, more tender. Every Christian, whether married, single or celibate is called to live a life of love. While repression works against such a life, suppression can be a powerful integrating force that helps us to direct our lives toward helping others. Our sexuality should be neither denied nor feared but rather consciously integrated into our personalities so that we can be more human and more loving, which is to say more holy.

A Christian cannot seriously reflect on the mystery of

sexuality without considering the virtue of chastity. Strange that even as I write the word "chastity" all sorts of negative images and ideas come into my mind. Chastity is a virtue and it deals predominantly not with what we should not do but with how we should live. Because sexuality is such an important part of our personalities, and therefore should be an important part of our spiritualities, chastity must play a key role in our Christian lives. Unfortunately people continue to confuse chastity with other realities that it is not. To be chaste is not identical with celibacy or virginity. All Christians are called to be chaste, married Christians and unmarried, celibate and non-celibate, virgins and those who are not virgins. To be a Christian is to be called to be chaste. Chastity does not mean the absence of or denial of sexuality but rather the proper use of sexuality. Every person is going to live a sexual life if he or she is to be human. Chastity is the virtue which directs our sexuality.

Some of the best writing I have encountered on chastity is in Donald Goergen's wonderful book *The Sexual Celibate* (A Crossroad Book, The Seabury Press, New York, 1974). I think it is very significant that the chapter in which he discusses chastity Goergen entitles "Chastity and Tactility." Chastity does not direct us never to touch people but rather directs us to the proper use of touch. There are times when a hug or an embrace or a kiss is proper and good and holy. Just as the virtue of temperance does not direct us to stop eating and drinking but rather helps us to eat and drink properly, chastity does not direct us to be non-sexual but rather directs our sexuality properly. Goergen writes:

"Chastity is that virtue concerned with the integration of sexuality into our lives as Christians. It is important because sexuality is important. If sexuality were insignificant to our lives as human beings, we would not have to be so concerned about chastity. *Chastity is that virtue which helps us to utilize the totality of our sexuality and put it at the service of our becoming Christian.* It brings together the sexual and the spiritual. Chastity does not integrate the two by denying or negating one while affirming or positing the other. It affirms both." (p.96)

Chastity, like all the virtues, is at the service of love. Contrary to a popular image, chastity does not make us cold or unloving but rather more loving, and indeed more passionate lovers. Chastity does this for married people, single people and celibates. The power for relationship that is contained within our sexuality receives direction from the virtue of chastity.

It is especially sad to me that when theater or film or television comedy or drama wish to portray a cleric they often opt for a dried up, rigid, naive, cold person. Chastity works against all those negative characteristics. Chastity should lead to the fulfillment of human personality not the destruction of personality. People who are chaste should be the most attractive people in the world because they are people who are living the human mystery most profoundly, they are people whose lives are directed toward loving.

It strikes me that chastity is a virtue that can enable Christians to be special signs in the contemporary world. All around us, in novels, plays, films and on television, we see the trivialization of sex. The key word seems to be pleasure and any more profound meaning to sex seems to be absent. The married Christian who lives up to his or her marriage vows and who refuses to be unfaithful can be a tremendous sign in contemporary society. The single Christian, who lives chastely and refuses to sin sexually even though he or she is told everyone does it, can be a terrific witness to his or her contemporaries. The celibate who has forsaken the tremendous blessing of married life but who is still a loving, caring, warm, compassionate person can be a sign of God's love to others.

Though some people do not realize it, everyone is looking for signs of the Divine in their lives. People need assurance that in spite of appearances, in spite of trials and sufferings, there is meaning to human living, that God never abandons us. God speaks to us in many ways. One way is through other people. A marvelous sign of God's presence in the world is the loving, caring, unselfish person. Such people remind us of what human existence ultimately means. The chaste person can and should be such a sign.

I do not really remember when I began to link friendship and spirituality in my own mind. Certainly my training in college and in the seminary did not foster such a link. In my seminary training there was strong discouragement of what were referred to as "particular friendships." What was being discouraged, I think, were cliques and relationships that were so exclusive that they violated the charity that ought to pervade a seminary. Unfortunately the beauty of a deep friendship and indeed the salvific power of a deep friendship may have been overlooked. Certainly deep friendships were not encouraged. Yet if our religion is incarnational and if the salvific death and resurrection of Jesus have transformed everything and enabled us to find God in our everyday lives then what in our everyday lives could be a better and richer place to find God than our friendships?

Whenever I am asked about the blessings in my life, one of the first that comes to mind is my experience of friendship. I have been enormously blessed throughout my life with wonderful friends. It is not as though I have done something to earn such friendships; my entire experience of friendships is that they have been gifts. I can recall years ago having a conversation with a friend of mine who had left the priesthood and with his wife. The topic of celibacy came up and my friend's wife said to me, "You seem very happy, Bob. How has that happened?" The impression I received from her question and from the way she asked it was that she found it very difficult to imagine how a person could be celibate and be happy. She knew a number of ex-religious and I guess that celibacy was cited so often to her as the reason for leaving the priesthood and the religious life that she could not understand how any celibate could be happy. I suspected that she thought that celibate existence must be unbearably lonely and really a humanly impossible way to live. Immediately I said, "I have been blessed with great friends." As soon as I made the statement I began to wonder why that was the first thing that I said in response to her question. Why did I think of friendships as one of the most important contributions to my happiness? Now close to twenty years later, I think I see a wisdom in my answer. If loving and being loved are what human life is all about, then what is more important than our friendships? What is more valuable, what a greater treasure? What is a greater sign of God's presence in our lives?

In *By Way of the Heart: Toward a Holistic Christian Spirituality* Wilkie Au stresses the importance of friendship in Christian living. He writes:

> "Unfortunately, some Christians still need to be convinced of the value of friendship in Christian living. For example, a spirituality that privatizes one's relationship with God, expressed in a 'Jesus-and-me' mentality, easily slips into viewing friendship as superfluous. 'With Jesus as my friend, I don't need anyone else' reflects such an outlook. Directly or indirectly, this way of thinking was for years instilled in priests and religious, who were warned that deep human friendship could weaken the intensity of their relationship with Christ and also endanger their vow of chastity." (p.44)

There is a kind of spirituality which seems to stress that people can be obstacles to our relationship with God. If there ever was a time when that type of spirituality appealed to me, it is long gone. At this point in my life I find it very unattractive. How could the most beautiful creature that God has created on earth, the human person, be anything but a sign of God?

I believe that God has been revealed to us through Jesus, God's Son. But God is also revealed through other realities such as beautiful sunsets, mountains, and rivers. I think that God is also revealed in the animal kingdom. Everything that exists is precisely because God loves it. When God loves, that love is creative. God's love makes things be! Everything that is, even the smallest insect is because of God's love. Everything that God has created is like a word or message from God, speaking to those who have ears to hear and revealing to those who have eyes to see the wonders and beauty and goodness of the Divine.

God is love. Human friendship is about loving and being loved. How could human friendship not be one of the most important realities in our spirituality? Through human friendships we encounter God.

Unfortunately the pressures of contemporary society can work against friendship. To develop deep friendships takes time and effort, involves sacrifices and even requires people to "waste time" together. It is easy to have acquaintances but it is not easy to have friends. Yet what is more important than friendships? One of the main causes of the breakup of so many marriages is that the husband and wife never became friends. Without a marriage being a friendship what depth can the married couple reach in their union? In marriage preparation courses when the importance of communication is stressed what is really being said is that the man and woman should develop the deepest friendship that they can with one another.

In his *By Way of the Heart* Wilkie Au offers some marvelous insights into friendship. One that I never thought of previously is that one way for an individual to evaluate his or her chastity is to evaluate his or her friendships. What a person's friendships are like can provide insights into the person's chastity or lack of chastity. Noting that chaste people with effort and time have learned to put their sexuality at the service of love and personal development and that as a result they are capable of greater openness toward others and greater commitment to others, Au writes:

> "Viewing others as irreducible wholes, they find themselves increasingly incapable of abusing others for their own selfish sexual interests. Chastity is the measure of

one's capacity as a woman or a man to love others as women and men. To gauge how chaste we are, a good practical guideline is the depth and quality of our friendships. To remain at a safe distance from others is not a sign of chastity. On the contrary, it is a kind of unchastity if it prevents us from involving ourselves deeply and caringly in others' lives." (p.150)

What Au writes makes a great deal of sense, especially if we remind ourselves that our sexuality has within it a tremendous power for relationships. Chastity enables a person to use that power for love.

Of course our model in probing the mystery of friendship, as for everything else in our Christian stories, is Jesus. He had an enormous capacity for friendship. Whether we think about the way he related to his disciples, or the way he related to the woman who washed his feet and dried them with her hair, or the way he related to the Samaritan woman at the well, or the way he related to Mary and Martha, we have a model of how men and women should be treated. Jesus never uses or abuses or manipulates or dominates anyone. He has a warm, caring attitude toward everyone and apparently that very attitude made him extremely attractive to people.

Perhaps nothing so illuminates the most profound meaning of friendship both in the story of Jesus and in our story as the last supper Jesus had with his friends. After washing his apostles' feet, a beautiful sign of his love for them and a beautiful example of how they should love others, Jesus said:

"This is my commandment, that you love one another as I have loved you. Greater love than this no one has, that one lay down his life for his friends. You are my friends if you do the things I command you. No longer do I call you servants, because the servant does not know what his master does. But I have called you friends, because all things that I have heard from my Father I have made known to you." (Jn 15:12-15)

Jesus is calling his apostles into an intimate union of love with him and with his Father. Later at this supper he will give them his flesh to eat and his blood to drink. Jesus also is calling us into an intimate union with him and his Father. He also has given us his flesh to eat and his blood to drink. The Son of God wants to have an intimate love relationship with each of us. At the center of Jesus' story is the eucharist and it also should be at the center of our stories.

In our efforts to grow closer to God, in our efforts to make the story of our lives a Christ-centered story, we have many realities that help us. Each of us could make a list of people and events that have had a profound influence on us. The presence of the Risen Christ in the eucharist is one of the great gifts that God has given us. The eucharist is the Word of God and that Word tells us not only who God is but who we are. That Word reveals that our lives should be love stories.

Questions

1. Can you articulate a Christian view of sexuality?

2. How does your sexuality relate to your spirituality?

3. Do you believe that you will never be loved more by God than at this moment? What implications can you draw from your answer?

4. How do your friendships figure into your sexuality and spirituality?

5. How does chastity fit into a married person's life? into a single person's life? into a celibate person's life? into your life?

I say more: the just man justices;
Keeps grace: that keeps all his goings graces;
Acts in God's eye what in God's eye he is—
Christ—for Christ plays in ten thousand places,
Lovely in limbs, and lovely in eyes not his
To the Father through the features of men's faces.

—Gerard Manley Hopkins

Chapter III

THE MYSTERY OF THE SELF

RECENTLY WHILE I WAS SPEAKING about the mystery of love during a eucharistic celebration, a scene from a Walker Percy novel popped into my head. The novel was *The Thanatos Syndrome* (Farrar, Straus, Giroux, New York, l987). The scene was the one in which the novel's hero, Dr. Thomas More, visits Father Smith, a Catholic priest who has withdrawn from society and lives up in a tower, seemingly modelling himself on St. Simon Stylites. The priest is conducting his own protest against a death-dealing society. The villains of the novel, who are trying to create a behavioristic society that will function more efficiently than one in which people exercise their freedom, have urged Dr. More to find out what the priest is doing.

While interviewing Father Smith, Dr. More asks if he still says Mass and the priest answers that he does. Then Dr. More asks if he preaches, and the priest answers that he can't because the secular society has worn away all the profound meanings that religious words once had. As that scene came to me, I think I understood the point that Percy was making in a way that I had not understood it previously. I had a personal experience of the problem that Percy was unveiling.

How can you speak about love in a society that has bought into consumerism? How can you preach about love when the meaning of the word today seems to foster narcissism? How can you present the Christian ideal of loving God and neighbor when the images of love that society promotes are sentimental and even selfish?

Often while thinking of the romantic and excessively emotional images of love presented by our society I think of a profound insight into love from Dostoevsky's *The Brothers Karamazov*. Dorothy Day, the co-founder of the Catholic Worker, liked the insight very much. In the novel the insight is articulated by Father Zosyma. The insight is that "love in action is a harsh and dreadful thing compared to love in words," and yet love is the heart and soul of Christianity. The idea that love is a harsh and dreadful thing is about as far from our society's depiction of love as possible.

My own view of love is that loving always involves dying to self. Some people who live lives of great unselfishness may come to find loving easy, but I suspect most of us sinners never find dying to self easy. But is there a special problem in our society as the twentieth century comes to an end? I suspect that there is. Why else would marriage be in such a sad state in this country? Could it be that we have a kind of "epidemic" a widespread inability to love deeply? I don't know, but I wonder. Could it be that some people in our society are incapable of loving? I don't know, but I wonder.

My own view of love, and of course I could be wrong, is that people do not either fall in love or fall out of love. I believe that though we may have enormously strong emotions moving us in one direction or the other, we love whom we freely choose to love and we do not love whom we freely choose not to love. In my view, love is not a feeling but a choice. We can fall in or out of feelings, but love is a free choice.

It bothers me that some people speak about their decisions springing from love when actually their decisions involve the neglect of duties toward someone else. In other words the word "love," which should imply an unselfishness, is used to justify a self-centeredness. The word "love" is used to mean almost the opposite of what it should mean. I have even heard people use love to justify adultery.

As I gave my homily on love that day, I found myself looking for dramatic images. I was trying to say something new and different. As I spoke I felt the need to stir both the congregation and myself. In the middle of the homily I mentioned that in talking about love I wished that I could invent some new words because what we were reflecting on was so important that it seemed to require a unique set of words.

I am not sure about my perception of the "epidemic," but I know that all of us who are involved in the education of people must try to call people to unselfishness. Anything less is not worthy of persons.

We are also called to serious self-reflection. In trying to make sense of our lives, of our stories, it is necessary to engage in some deep self-reflection. There are signs that large numbers of people no longer can reflect with any depth about anything serious.

I first became aware of some people's inability to reflect seriously about problems while I was preparing people for marriage and also while doing some marriage counselling. As I tried to involve some engaged couples in the discussion of serious topics related to their future married life, I saw how difficult this was for them. No matter what topic I introduced, they seemed unable to engage in a serious discussion or to offer any insights into how the topic related to their future life together. Also while trying to help people with marriage problems, I noticed that some people could not face a problem, reflect on it, and then take steps to deal with it. In trying to patch up marriages that are on the brink of breaking, I often wonder, after listening to the husband and wife describe their relationship, whether they ever loved one another. But I also wonder whether they have ever thought deeply about the meaning of love. I have come to suspect that many people have either no or only the most superficial understanding of what love is. Amazed and disturbed by my experience with a number of engaged couples, I spoke with a priest who does more marriage counselling than I and his experience was almost exactly the same as mine.

As someone who teaches philosophy at the largest Catholic university in the country, I may be especially sensitive to an apparent inability of some people to engage in serious reflection. I meet many people who never seem to have thought seriously about truth, about whether truth exists and whether we can reach it and articulate it. The most naive relativism seems to be accepted by many. The notion that truth is made up arbitrarily by us is popular even among people who have college degrees. Because I believe correct thinking about truth, especially about the truth related to the self, is crucially important, I am surprised that some universities in the United States bestow college degrees on students who have never taken a philosophy course. How can someone who has never had to think seriously about truth receive a college diploma? How can such a person be considered educated?

The Depth of Self

There are levels of myself that I cannot clearly grasp. The more deeply I enter into self-understanding, the more depth I discover in myself. John Haught has articulated this experience of depth well in *What Is God?*

"There is always more to me than is contained in my impressions of myself. My 'self-image' does not exhaust what I am. I need not be an expert in depth psychology in order to validate this observation. I need only a little experience of living to be able to see its truth. Looking back a few years, or even a few months or days, I remember that I thought I knew who I was. But new experiences have reshaped my life. New questions, new feelings and moods, new dreams and fantasies, new expectations of myself have intervened. I now know that I am not what I thought I was. I may assume at this moment that I am not exactly what I seem to be to myself or to others." (pp. 11-12)

I believe that at this point in my life I understand myself better than I have ever understood myself previously. Comments that were made to me by close friends over the last thirty years, which I thought I understood at the time, I now understand in a new way. How has this growth in self-understanding happened? It seems that my growth in self-understanding has come partly through my reading, study, and self-reflection; partly through being loved by close friends and partly by loving close friends; partly in some strange way by writing a weekly column in a Catholic newspaper; partly through a long relationship with a spiritual director; partly through the process of aging.

That I may have grown in self-understanding through reading, study and self-reflection is not surprising, especially since my field is philosophy. The great questions of life are put before us in philosophy and it is difficult to avoid serious self-reflection as we ponder the meaning of life, of death, of love. To do philosophy properly is to be confronted by the mystery of the self.

The experience of being loved and the experience of loving are special in their power to provide insight into self. When people love us, they affirm us, heal us, create us. Babies, who are not loved, die; adults, who are not loved, are in danger of withering psychologically. Those who love us are telling us the most profound truth about ourselves: that we are lovable. When we love we have a chance of discovering a great truth about human existence: unselfishness leads to happiness.

The experience of writing a weekly column for more than twenty-five years has in some mysterious way helped me to understand myself better though I am not sure how it happened. The pressure of a weekly writing assignment calls you to reflection and, at least indirectly, it calls you to self-reflection. Perhaps it is the challenge of revealing yourself through your writing to readers you don't know and whom you may never meet. Over the years my weekly columns seem to have become more personal. Apparently I have been revealing myself in the column more than I realized. Frequently when I am a guest lecturer somewhere people come up to me after the lecture and say something like "I feel as though I know you. I have been reading your column for years and you reveal a great deal of yourself in the column."

I understand myself better through my relationship

with my spiritual director. He has been available for me, has listened to me and has guided me for twenty-five years. That cross alone should gain him heaven! Being as honest as I can be with him has enabled me to discover all sorts of truths about myself. A very dedicated priest, he is a person with considerable psychological insight. His understanding, affirming presence in my life has been a marvelous creative gift. Through his support and encouragement I have been able to understand what previously confused me, to face what previously frightened me, to work through what previously crippled me. His presence has been a living sign of God's loving presence. Simply put, he has liberated me.

If my growth in self-understanding has been partly a product of the process of aging then I guess I have become not only older but wiser. I hope so. Growth in self-understanding is a marvelous experience that can make us more free and more at peace. God's loving presence can change us in many ways. One way is by freeing us to grow in self-understanding.

The Pope, Positivism and Persons

Pope John Paul II was a professor of philosophy and so his statements often reveal his profound philosophical background. Amidst the confusion of the contemporary world the Pope's ability to reflect deeply on the mystery of person can provide special illumination for people who are trying to make sense of their lives.

Anyone who believes that philosophy or ideas are of no real significance, that as Christians we should be involved in what it more practical, in what is more immediate, should read *Crossing the Threshold of Hope* (Alfred A. Knopf, New York, 1994). The Pope's approach underlines the truth that eventually the ideas in the books of the great philosophers trickle down and for better or worse influence and affect people who never read those books or even heard of those thinkers. The Pope's comments on the existence of God can remind us that we create our stories with God. The God in whom Christians believe is not a distant bystander. The Christian God is Love—totally involved in our stories.

In an early section of the book the Pope makes several important points about the existence of God. The Holy Father wants to emphasize the importance of thinking about God and of seeing the validity of this thinking. He stresses that we have been trapped into what he describes as a positivist mentality. Positivism is the philosophy which says that all we can know is the sensible, that the mind cannot get beyond what can be seen or touched or tasted or smelled or heard. For the positivist the empirical means what can be sensed. This attitude has been widespread, and the Pope is justly concerned about it. According to the positivist mentality, talk about God is meaningless. The Pope writes:

"Positivism has not only been a philosophy or a methodology; it has been one of those schools of suspicion that the modern era has seen grow and prosper. Is man truly capable of knowing something beyond what he sees with his eyes or hears with his ears? Does some kind of knowledge other than the strictly empirical exist? Is the human capacity for reason completely subject to the senses and internally directed by the laws of mathematics, which have been shown to be particularly useful in the rational ordering of phenomena and for guiding technical progress?

"If we put ourselves in the positivist perspective concepts such as God or the soul simply lose meaning. In terms of sensory experience, in fact, nothing corresponds to God or the soul." (p.33)

Pope John is profoundly correct to attack the positivist mentality. As long as it continues, religion cannot be given any importance or indeed any credence. That it should be attacked by the Pope, who is a professional philosopher, adds weight to the indictment.

Questions

1. Do you think of yourself as a mystery? of your loved ones as mysteries? of God as a mystery?

2. How do you understand selflessness as it relates to marriage?

3. How does truth relate to spirituality and friendship?

Once there was a friend.
He watched me from the sky.
Maybe he never lived at all.
Maybe too much friendship made him die.

When the gang played cops-and-robbers in the alley
It was my friend who told me which were which.
Now he doesn't tell me any more.
(Which team am I playing for?)...

Every time I stood upon a crossroads,
It made me mad to feel him watch me choose.
I'm glad there's no more spying while I play.
Still, I'm sad he went away.

—PETER VIERECK

Chapter IV

WHERE IS GOD?

IN A SECTION of *Crossing the Threshold of Hope* Pope John
Paul II deals specifically with the question, "Why does
God not reveal himself more clearly?" After I saw this sec-
tion in the Pope's book, I thought of the opening scene in
Woody Allen's film, *Husbands and Wives*. In the film Allen
is watching a philosopher speak on television. The philo-
sopher is speaking about science and quotes Einstein as
having pointed to the order in the world with the state-
ment, "God does not play dice with the universe." The
Woody Allen character responds to the television set,
"No. He plays hide and seek." Though I have never met
Allen I suspect that this is his view, namely, that he wishes
God was more clear in his self-revelation, that God did
not "hide" from us.

To someone who is trying to find God this has to be a
terribly important question. I like the way that the Pope
handles it. The Pope starts by pointing out that the question comes out of a contemporary agnosticism, not a mil-
itant atheism. The question thrives in an atmosphere of
doubt and confusion and in a sense reechoes questions in
the Old and New Testament.

What must be emphasized is that God is radical mystery and, because of our limited minds, will always be
radical mystery in relation to us. There is no way that we
are going to understand God the way we understand a
scientific problem. This does not mean that we cannot

know God at all but that we can never understand God completely. The Pope asks whether God could have gone further in his stooping down to us, in his drawing near to us. Then the Pope writes:

> "From one point of view, it is right to say that God revealed too much of Himself to man, too much of that which is most divine, that which is His intimate life. He revealed Himself in His Mystery. He was not mindful of the fact that such an *unveiling would in a certain way obscure Him in the eyes of man, because man is not capable of with-standing an excess of the Mystery.* He does not want to be pervaded and overwhelmed by it. Yet, man knows that God is the One in whom 'we live and move and have our being' (Acts 17:28); but why must that be confirmed by His Death and Resurrection? Yet St. Paul writes, 'If Christ has not been raised, then empty is our preaching; empty, too, your faith.'" (1 Cor 15:14) (p. 41)

What the Pope is saying is that God is not hiding but rather wants us to know and love him. What more would we like God to do that would make it easier for us to know and love him? Miracles? He did them and some did not believe. Apparitions? He did them and some did not believe. Voices? We still would have to decide whether the voices are authentic or whether we are hallucinating. I believe that God has done more than enough for us to know him and love him. God sent his Son and is constantly sending his graces to help us believe and love.

My own opinion is that when someone sincerely seeks God, there is a sense in which that person has already found God, even if that person cannot consciously make an act of faith. Why do I say that? Because God is madly in love with each and every one of us. God is not hiding from us but rather pursuing us. God loves each and every one of us, the "believers" and "unbelievers" more than any one of us loves himself or herself.

In *Crossing the Threshold of Hope* Pope John Paul II makes several important and profound points about prayer. I have come to believe that our prayer life is a very good indication of our relationship with God. How we pray can tell us what our view of ourselves is. Prayer is the key way that we create our stories with God. Prayer is the most important interaction between God and us.

I would describe the Pope's view of prayer as cosmic. The Pope's philosophical background in personalism is suggested in what he says about prayer. The Holy Father writes:

> "What is prayer? It is commonly held to be a conversation. In a conversation there are always an 'I' and a 'thou' or 'you'. In this case the 'Thou' is with a capital T. If at first the 'I' seems to be the most important element at prayer, prayer teaches that the situation is actually different. The 'Thou' is more important because our prayer begins with God. In his letter to the Romans, Saint Paul teaches precisely this. According to the apostle, prayer reflects all created reality; it is in a certain sense a cosmic function." (p. 16)

In prayer we are playing our role in speaking for the rest of creation. The Pope refers to human persons as the priests of all creation. We are never more priests than when we are praying, offering ourselves in love to our Father, and through our self-offering also presenting the rest of creation to our Father. The most obvious and powerful example of this is the Eucharist. Through the bread and wine, not only we, but all of creation is offered up to God.

The Pope's view of prayer and creation has a special appeal to me because it kills all dualisms. Unfortunately some Christians in their understanding of the Christian life have thought of religion in excessively narrow terms. They have thought of one section of their lives, probably the time spent in church or at prayer, as religious and the rest of their lives as secular. The Pope's vision destroys that view. If Christians are the priests of creation, then everything that we do can become part of our prayer. Nothing need escape the power of Christ's redemptive grace nor our attempts at offering creation back to our Father. To believe that we are the priests of creation is to believe that we are called to battle the sin that stains creation and to foster the love that ought to permeate God's creation.

The dialogue between God and creation which passes through us as priests begins with God lovingly speaking to us and inviting us into relationship. Prayer starts because of God's commitment to us. Prayer also reveals our commitment to God. Recalling this should make us humble, grateful and joyful. Humble because we have nothing of value which we have not received. Grateful because the God who holds the universe in existence wishes to enter into an intimate loving relationship with us. Joyful because God's love for us is so great that it is beyond our imagining. It really is awesome that God should want an intimate relationship with us. No matter how frequently or how profoundly we reflect on God's desire to have a love relationship with us it should never cease to cause us to marvel and wonder. If this is not good news, then what is?

Personalist Philosophy

My own reading, study and reflection in philosophy have been greatly gifted through the philosophy of personalism. About ten years ago at St. John's University I created an elective course entitled Personalism. Through that course I was able to read and reflect on some of the most beautiful and inspiring philosophy ever created. It is a philosophy that has deeply influenced Pope John Paul's thinking. One of the great twentieth century philosophers whose thought I teach in the course is Gabriel Marcel (1889-1973).

Marcel reflects on human experience, especially certain important human experiences such as the experience of taking a vow or making a commitment or trusting or loving another and constructs his philosophy from his reflections on these experiences. One way to characterize Marcel's thought is to say that it is the complete opposite of what is emphasized in contemporary society. In fact Marcel's thought might be looked on as a reaction to many of the false values that have been promoted in Western society during this century.

Marcel is opposed to what has come to be called scientism, which is the view that only positive science, such as physics, chemistry and biology, can reach the truth. My own experience is that an enormous number of Americans, at least implicitly, embrace scientism. For several years I taught religion at a secular college. At the beginning of the course none of the students believed that religion had anything to do with the truth, that if you wanted to know truth you checked with science. They seemed to think of religion as dealing with feelings, as being completely subjective and unrelated to truth. Eventually they came to see that there are many ways of reaching the truth and that religion is definitely one of those ways.

Marcel was also concerned with the dangers of technology, especially with the danger of persons becoming subordinate to machines, of persons coming to believe that their salvation and human fulfillment would come through machines. Of course technology is marvelous, but it has to be put at the service of persons rather than have persons put at the service of it. Marcel was concerned that our preoccupation with machines would move us toward thinking of persons as highly developed machines.

In one of this writings Marcel says that the more a person trusts in technology the more likely the person is to despair. Marcel suggests that this is the normal outcome of looking for salvation through technology. Things will never fulfill us, and things cannot save us. Unfortunately the consumer society keeps telling us that they can, and it is easy to be seduced by the messages that tell us that our value as persons is in our possessions.

Marcel's philosophical vision is a wonderful antidote to the superficial and false images of self that bombard us in contemporary society. Marcel's philosophy reminds us that our value is tied to our relationship with an Other.

I suppose what I most like about the philosophy of Gabriel Marcel is that his philosophy is rooted in human experience and that from human experience Marcel is able to draw the most marvelous insights into human nature. Two examples come to mind immediately.

One example is Marcel's observation that the very fact that people make marriage vows suggests that there must be a God. The other example is Marcel's suggestion that, in loving, the lover discovers that the beloved is immortal. I like both examples. If there is no God, then marriage vows make no sense at all. In fact they are silly. It makes no sense to make an unconditional vow to a conditioned, finite being. Why should one person promise to stay with another person no matter what happens? The person to whom the vow is being made is a weak, limited person who might change dramatically. Why would anyone make unconditional vows to a person who might seriously disappoint, who might not live up to the expectations of the one making the vow? Marriage vows are foolish unless there is an unconditional being who will support the one making the vow. Only if there is a God who will support and encourage us does a statement of committing "for better or worse, for richer or poorer, in sickness and in health, until death" make any sense. Without God the person making the vow is putting impossible expectations on the beloved. Why would anyone make an unlimited promise to a limited being? Perhaps it is the absence of God in people's consciousness that makes so many think that "trial marriages" are a good idea and that no one should ever say "forever." In other words, the so-called "death of God" culture that we live in has at least indirectly contributed to the lack of commitment we observe in many marriages. Half-consciously some people may be thinking a life-long commitment makes no sense. If there is no God, they are correct!

The second example also appeals to me a great deal. Marcel suggests that through loving the lover finds out that the beloved will live forever. I agree completely. If there is no life beyond the grave, then human love is counterfeit and a fraud. Whenever one person says to another, "I love you," implicit in that statement is the notion that the lover will love the beloved forever. It is absolutely impossible to intend to love someone for a time. Even to try to articulate such love reveals how impossible it is: "I will love you for this weekend" or "I will love you for the next three months." Whenever a person loves, that person intends to love forever. The person may choose at some point in time to stop loving, but when the person does love, the intention is to love forever.

I am reminded of a dramatic event that suggests the truth of Marcel's insight. A Catholic married couple I know had two close friends, a married couple, who were secular humanists. Often the two couples would have discussions about whether there was or was not a God and whether there was a life beyond the grave. The secular humanists, who were wonderful people, insisted there was no God nor any life but the one on this earth. When the female secular humanist died, my friends went to the memorial service. They said to the widower, "We have just been to Mass and received the body and blood of Jesus for you and your wife. We are praying for you." The widower thanked them and through tears said, "Do you think that what you believe might be the truth?" Why did he say that? I think that he said it because he had some sense that his wife could not be gone forever, that his entire experience of loving her promised eternity, and death seemed to contradict that experience.

I suppose that what I like most about Marcel is that his insights are accessible to anyone. It is not necessary that we go to some library and read philosophical tomes. All that is necessary is that we reflect on important experiences in our lives. In other words that we reflect on our stories.

Questions

1. In your experience have you come upon the positivism the Pope opposes?
2. Is God difficult to find?
3. Do you know some non-believers who seem holier and closer to God than some believers?
4. Is your self-understanding good and is it improving? What has contributed to your self-understanding?
5. Do marriage vows or any life commitments reveal God's presence?
6. Does love increase our awareness of the immortality of persons?

...Enough! the Resurrection,
A heart's-clarion! Away grief's gasping,
joyless days, dejection.
Across my foundering deck shone
A beacon, an eternal beam
Flesh fade, and moral trash
Fall to the residuary worm;
world's wildfire, leave but ash:
In a flash, at a trumpet crash,
I am all at once what Christ is,
since he was what I am, and
This Jack, joke, poor potsherd,
patch, matchwood, immortal diamond,
Is immortal diamond.

—GERARD MANLEY HOPKINS

Chapter V

Jesus' Story: Our Model

EACH OF US has subplots in his or her life. What we are striving for is an integration. But to achieve the most profound integrity in our lives requires more than merely unifying the activities in our lives. For us to achieve a deep integrity in our lives, our stories need to be modeled on the story of Jesus.

The essence of Jesus' story lies not in the externals but in the inner dispositions of Jesus, in the heroism and love that characterized Jesus' life. In order to model our stories on Jesus' story, we do not need to speak the language that Jesus spoke or live in that area of the world in which Jesus lived. We need to model our consciousness on Jesus' consciousness, our relationship with God on Jesus' relationship with God, our concern and compassion for others on Jesus' concern and compassion for others. We want the Risen Christ to live within us through grace, and we want to act out in our lives the pattern of Jesus' death and resurrection.

Let's imagine Jesus' experience in the Garden of Gethsemane. I think of him on the brink of despair. It must have seemed to him that everything was lost. He had been misunderstood by his friends and one of those friends had betrayed him for money. He must have felt abandoned and terribly alone. Each of us will be called in our stories to feel something like the dark night of

Gethsemane. We may feel abandoned and terribly alone. It is possible that in our stories those feelings will be especially strong as we approach our death. Each of us will be called to surrender our lives to God our Father as Jesus was called. Waiting for us, if we make that surrender, is the victory won by Jesus.

I find Holy Week the most dramatic week of the year because in special ways it celebrates very dramatic events in Jesus' story, and the Church invites us to go through those events with our Risen Lord. Through sign and sacrament the Church during Holy Week commemorates the most important events in the story of Jesus, indeed in the story of the human race. In Holy Week we liturgically celebrate the story of salvation.

Each of us must take responsibility for his or her story. But we do not write our story alone. God is lovingly present through the Risen Christ at every moment of our story inviting us to a deeper love relationship. Life is an adventure filled with risk, and the greatest risk is loving.

Story, Self and Suffering

Recently I have heard about several people suffering terribly which has caused me to think about the presence of the cross in people's lives. Jesus' statement to the Apostles has also been on my mind: "If anyone wants to be a follower of mine, let him renounce himself and take up his cross every day and follow me. For anyone who wants to save his life will lose it; but anyone who loses his life for my sake, that man will save it." (Luke 9:23,24)

In light of human experience and the words of Jesus, what meaning can a cross have in the life of a Christian?

What role can the cross play in our stories?

I do not think we should go looking for crosses or asking God to send them to us. Life provides crosses for most of us. We become physically sick; or we experience emotional problems or severe disappointment in relation to hopes, plans and dreams. We and those we love grow older and eventually we will all die.

Somehow in the mystery of God's providence, suffering can purify us and lead us closer to God. More than forty years ago when I was a seminarian I can recall hearing a priest, who experienced enormous suffering in his life, talk about suffering. During the time I knew him he had several breakdowns. He knew suffering first hand. He told me about visiting someone in the hospital who was dying. The priest said that he spoke to the dying person about the mystery of suffering and about the suffering person's union with Christ. The priest said that the dying person seemed to grasp some of what he was trying to communicate. I did not completely grasp what the priest meant then and though I understand it better now I still find it quite mysterious how suffering can draw people closer to God.

The believer who is suffering can unite with the sufferings of Christ and the power of Jesus' death and resurrection can profoundly affect the person who is in pain. We need not suffer like animals, ignorant of any possible meaning or role that suffering may have in our lives. We believe that suffering because of Jesus's death and resurrection can be redemptive.

All the crosses I have mentioned thus far are crosses that are delivered to us by life. There are other crosses that come to us precisely because we are Christians. I think this is directly related to the words of Jesus from Luke's gospel. Christian crosses may take varied forms but what is common to them is that they are present because a person is following Christ. The cross may be the failure to advance in business because you are trying to imitate the honesty of Jesus even though you know other people are advancing dishonestly. The cross may be being faithful to your marriage vows even though many around you are violating theirs. The cross may be living a single life of chastity even though you live in a society which seems to promote the opposite. The cross may be due to a choice of a vocation in which you serve people rather than pursue power, fame or money. What makes a cross Christian is that it exists because of a commitment to Christ.

Christians follow a God who died on a cross and I think that means that somehow you have to climb up on the cross with Him. There does not seem to be any easy way to be saved. If we reflect on our stories I think we will discover that following Jesus costs us something.

Death: Freedom and Fulfillment

One of the most interesting ideas that I find in the writings of contemporary theologians concerning death is that death can be an individual's most free action. This notion is in the excellent chapter on death in John Sachs' *The Christian Vision of Humanity: Christian Anthropology* (Liturgical Press, Collegeville, MN, 1991). Ordinarily we don't think of death as a free choice except when that death is a suicide. But a death sums up all the free choices that a person makes. A death sums up who a person is.

In our lives most of us make many free choices. With

each choice we are creating ourselves. Some contemporary philosophers speak of a human person as a self-project. By that they mean that each person is directing himself or herself into the future. Each choice, and especially the big decisions in an individual's life, give that life a direction and make the individual the person he or she is. No one stands still. If we look at ourselves from a religious point of view, then each of us is either moving toward God or away from God, and each of us is either moving toward becoming a saint or toward damnation. There is no standing still in the spiritual life.

Father Sachs points out that Jesus does not die "for us" in the sense that he does something in our place that we won't have to do. We still have to die. Because of Jesus' death, dying can now be an act of faith, hope and love instead of something just to be dreaded, feared and denied. In our death we are called to make a great act of surrender to God. Father Sachs writes:

> "The surrender of self in trusting love to the mystery of the other is the greatest challenge of life. It is at once terrifying and transfixing. It comes to its final concentration in dying. The Christian is invited to imagine death as the final, summing and consuming act of self-abandonment to the one Mystery who alone is worthy of such total trust and self-abandonment, God. It is abandonment both as the loving entrustment of what I have achieved and endured and as the entrustment of the deepened desire for the fullness of life which has never found its real fulfillment. Our dying, like our living, is fundamentally an act of faith as self-entrustment. It can be a moment of grace." (pp. 80-81)

I agree completely with Father Sachs that the greatest challenge of life is to surrender one's self in trust. We find it difficult to surrender ourselves even to those whom we love and who love us. Inability to surrender is one of the problems that causes so many marriages to break up. If we cannot surrender to another, then we cannot have a permanent love relationship.

We are called to surrender ourselves to God. I know I find this extremely difficult to do because I am a person who likes to be in control. When I was a seminary student my spiritual director told me that what was most important for me, if I was going to grow spiritually, was to trust in God. Intellectually I knew that he was correct, but it took me a very long time to make even a little progress in trusting. I still find it difficult to surrender to God but my hope is that when my turn comes to die, I, through the grace of the Holy Spirit, will be able to surrender. Each of us is called to surrender to the Father who is totally in love with us. We are called to do this throughout our lives but in a special way at the moment of death. Our dying should be our final act of surrender, our final trusting "Yes" to God's loving presence to us.

I especially like Father Sachs' statement that the Christian is invited to imagine death as the "final, summing and consuming act of self-abandonment." That is exactly what death should be. Death is not only the last act that a human being performs on this earth, but it is also an act that expresses exactly who I am. My death will be "mine" for better or worse. My death is my expression of myself in relation to God, which is the only expression and relation that ultimately counts. Who I am before God is who I am. Everything comes together at the moment of death—our story reaches its fulfillment.

How I live in relation to God will influence how I die in relation to God.

"What gives death its sting is something quite indepen-
dent of biological processes. It is sin (I Cor 15:56). Apart
from physical pain, perhaps what we fear and *humanly
suffer* in death is radical loneliness, being completely
isolated and cut off: not only from our loved ones but most
especially from God. The emptiness, hopelessness and
terror which mark death can be seen as manifestations of
human sin which, long before the moment of death, have
weakened and perhaps destroyed many of our life-giving
relationships. The absence or remoteness of God is a real
turning away from God. It is not a punishment inflicted by
God, but the inescapable consequence of sin itself, not only
of some 'original' sin, but of our real personal sins."
(p. 78)

It seems to me that Father Sachs has noted something
extremely important about our view of death. It sums up
much of what has been dramatized in literature, on the
stage and in film in recent years. At times it may seem as
though emptiness is the only experience that is being dramatized in contemporary stories. A feeling of emptiness
can be frightening. It can be a feeling that our lives do not
add up to much, that we have missed many important
opportunities, that we have not lived up to our potential,
that in spite of all that we may have accomplished, our
lives have been failures. The feeling of emptiness can be
strong even if others point to many wonderful aspects of
our lives. Awareness of these aspects may not be enough
to help us to overcome our feelings of emptiness especially as we face our death.

The experience of *loneliness* is an experience of feeling
that I do not matter, that I am not significant, that nobody
cares about me. Death seems to be an experience that I
must undergo alone, and so facing my death can make me

feel all alone in the universe, even abandoned.

The unknown aspects of death can cause terror. What will it be like? What will happen to us? How will we handle the experience of death? How will we let go of life?

As I think about emptiness, loneliness and terror in relation to death, I suspect that these were part of Jesus' experience in the Garden of Gethsemane and on the cross. How could they not have been if Jesus was truly human? Perhaps emptiness and loneliness were especially strong because of the abandonment that Jesus experienced when his friends ran out on him. If we take the Incarnation seriously, if we remind ourselves of Jesus' humanity and of his sensitive personality, then being abandoned must have been an especially hurtful experience for him. Jesus experienced emptiness, loneliness and terror not because of any sins he committed but because he took upon himself our humanity and our sins. Jesus is a model for us in everything and in a special way in death.

Jesus surrenders to his Father in death. This is what we are called to do in death but also in our life. To the extent that we can have a loving, intimate relationship with God our Father, to that extent we will be able to face our own death with confidence. Our trust and our confidence are not in ourselves. Alone we are lost. Our trust and our confidence are in our Father who loves us beyond our imagination.

Questions

1. How has and does Jesus' story influence your story?
2. How has the suffering of others influenced your story? How has your own suffering influenced your story?

3. Why is the cross necessary in every person's life?
4. How is death a surrender or an act of self-abandonment?

Faithful Love

There are days when I reflect
upon the moments of my history
and I taste satisfied fragrance,
like a well-aged bottle of wine.

There are other long-spent days
when I chew upon my memories,
only to taste the dry crumbs
of stale and molded bread.

There are yet other days
when I sit at a great distance,
looking at the life that is mine;
threading the loom of my past
with a deep belief in faithfulness.

It is then that I see how fidelity
has little to do with fine feelings,
and everything to do with deep trust,
believing the One who holds me in joy
will never let go when sorrow sets in.

—JOYCE RUPP

Chapter VI

HOW COMMITMENTS
WRITE OUR STORIES

PROBABLY NOTHING *writes* our stories more than our commitments. Teaching a philosophy course entitled "Personalism" at St. John's University moved me to rediscover a book that I had wanted to read more than fifteen years ago. The book is *Should Anyone Say Forever? On Making, Keeping and Breaking Commitments.* (Loyola University Press, Chicago, 1975) by John C. Haughey, S.J. Not only did the book help me to tie together many of the insights of personalist philosophers such as Gabriel Marcel, Martin Buber, Emmanuel Mounier and John Macmurray, but it helped me to see more deeply a connection between commitment and the meaning of personal existence.

You do not need to be a genius to know that permanent commitment has fallen on hard times. I suppose life commitments were never easy, but what is new to our age is the number of life commitments that are broken. The number of times that I have heard a married person say that he or she no longer wishes to be married astounds me. Before I was ordained a priest more than thirty-five years ago almost no one left the priesthood or the religious life. Of course it is possible that in the past many people stayed married or stayed in the priesthood or religious life because of social or ecclesiastical constraints. Whatever the reasons were or are, the topic of commitment is important and deserves reflection. Interpersonal commitment is at the heart of personal existence. Commitment reveals the mystery of person. It also shapes a person's story.

An example of lack of commitment is the person who wishes to keep his or her options open indefinitely. A superficial vision of freedom would see such a person as preserving his or her freedom. The contrary is true. We become persons through our commitments. Therefore the person who tries to avoid commitment is working against personal growth.

I find it fascinating that statistics show that people who live together before they make marital vows, have less of a chance to stay together than those who do not live together prior to marriage. I wonder why that is. Could it be that the period of "trial" means that the two people are using one another? Could it be that by trying one another out in a very intimate way they have made themselves less able to make a permanent commitment?

Certainly by not making commitments we make ourselves less free. Our commitments enormously color our future and give it a direction. Although we do not completely control the future, neither are we completely passive and helpless in the face of it. Our choices enormously influence the meaning of our future. Our choices shape our story.

Relating commitment to the narrow gate that Jesus urges people to pass through (Mt 7:13-14), Father Haughey in *Should Anyone Say Forever?* writes:

> "The narrow gate Jesus was alluding to probably refers to the gate in Jerusalem which could only accommodate people unaccompanied by their possessions and camels and donkeys. It was so small that it was a 'people only'

passageway. The metaphor suggests that life will be found only when a person is willing to particularize his choices in life and does so in such a way that he does not identify himself in terms of what he has or hopes to hold on to but in terms of who he is and who he intends to be present to. He chooses to enter the kingdom of persons and does so through particular people." (p. 21)

The idea that commitment is the way that we enter the kingdom of persons is beautiful. Without commitment we are on the sidelines of life, watching but not participating, observing but not contributing. If we avoid commitment, then we are looking for a free ride through life. There are no free rides. There is no way to avoid risk. By avoiding commitment we lose. This is another illustration of the profound insight that by dying we live, by giving ourselves away we reach a new level of self-possession. Through making life commitments our stories become adventures of love.

Reflecting on Commitments

One of the many marvelous insights in Father Haughey's book is that the less conscious one is of one's commitment the more likely it is that the person is content with it. If a person is always thinking about his or her commitment, always discussing it, then it seems likely that something is wrong. There is something in the person's experience that is calling the person to question, to analyze and perhaps even to doubt the value of the commitment. People who are happy in their permanent commitments ordinarily do not think about those commitments. They are living them and experiencing a great deal of fulfillment and so they do not feel a pressure to question or analyze. Rather than encouraging people to doubt or question their commitments, I am suggesting that we reflect on our commitments and look for the special presence of God in them. Even those of us who are happy in our commitments may profit from reflection on them. On my annual retreat I find reflection on my life commitment helps me to be more aware of the enormous blessings in my life. Through prayerful reflection I become more aware, not of what I have done for God, but of what God has done for me.

A person's permanent commitment does not lend itself to external observation. It involves the depth of the person who made it and so is to some extent inaccessible to anyone else. A permanent commitment is quite mysterious and impossible to completely understand. I will never understand myself completely, I will never understand God completely and so I will never understand my commitment completely nor will I ever understand my story completely. But the more truth we grasp about self, God, commitment and story, the more free we become.

Freedom and Commitment

One surefire way to destroy a marriage is to be jealous. The person who is jealous puts an impossible burden on his or her spouse. For the jealous person there is never enough love. Time and time again the jealous person wants proof that he or she is loved. Of course nothing that a spouse can do will ever convince a person who is extremely jealous. The fault is not with the spouse but with the jealous person. My observation is that jealousy often springs from an insecurity in the jealous person and a failure to accept their lovableness. I know that in the past I have had great difficulty trying to help jealous people.

I have come to see that not everyone is able to make a permanent commitment. Making permanent commitments is tied to being a person and requires some maturity and freedom. Anyone can articulate the words that express a vow, but not everyone can make a vow. We can get a parrot to say the words of a vow, but the parrot cannot really make a vow. The parrot is not free and does not know the meaning of the sounds that it is making. Only persons can make vows, and I have come to see that there are some persons who cannot make vows. I have come to see that some people are just not sufficiently free or self-possessed to make a life commitment. A level of maturity is required and some people have not reached that level.

The person who is lacking in self-possession, who is unable to freely direct his or her life, puts a terrible burden on a spouse. Such a person may be asking the spouse to fulfill him or her completely. Not being God, the spouse will not be able to do this. Instead of a mutual giving in love, one partner is being asked to make up for the psychological and perhaps spiritual deficiencies of the other. No one can live another person's life, not even in marriage.

I think that the increase in marriage annulments is a kind of blessing. Annulments remind us that it is no small achievement to stay married. They also show us that marriage takes preparation and maturity. Why is marriage in such a disastrous state in our society unless it be that personal maturity is lacking in our society? There is no easy, quick way to become psychologically mature or spiritually mature. Both types of maturity require sacrifice and a dying to self.

In our society a very popular view of freedom suggests that the more you keep your options open, the more free you are. Freedom is understood in terms of the variety of possibilities that are open to you and also in terms of the lack of responsibilities that you have. Unfortunately, responsibility is thought of as inimical to freedom, a commitment is thought of as the shrinking of freedom. The perfect expression of this outlook is the Playboy philosophy. The meaning of the philosophy is expressed well in the title of the magazine: *Playboy*. The whole idea of the philosophy is to keep males adolescent. Boys do not make commitments, only men do. The Playboy philosophy encourages males to play with women, to turn women into objects, to act as voyeurs in relation to women but never to make a commitment to a woman.

Free Commitments Write Our Stories

Freedom is a creative power that is meant to align us with God's will for us. What God wants for us is maximum freedom which is another way of saying what God wants for us is our holiness.

There is a meaning and direction to freedom which we can choose to act against. This may seem strange, but we can actually choose against our own freedom. The most obvious examples are a person taking drugs or drinking too much alcohol. In each instance the person's free choice to take drugs or drink excessively is actually destructive of the person's freedom. Another example of a person acting against his or her own freedom is the choice not to love or, even worse, the choice to hate. Hating not only hurts the person hated, but it also hurts the person who hates. The person hating is engaging in self-destructive activity and making himself or herself less free. Just as we can regress and become less free, we can progress and become more free. Freedom increases to the extent that it conforms to the meaning of personal existence.

The greater degree of freedom that a person achieves the easier virtuous acts become. The reason for this is that when a person loves deeply, what previously was very difficult may now be relatively easy. The virtue of charity has become so strong in a person who has achieved a deep freedom that what others find very difficult to do the loving person may find not very difficult at all. Think of Mother Teresa. The numerous acts of unselfishness that she has performed in her life achieved for her a degree of freedom that more selfish or self-centered people have not achieved.

The more I reflect on commitment the more I realize how mysterious commitment is, how mysterious freedom is and how mysterious we are. In relation to us God's freedom is loving and faithful. That's what we want our freedom to be, loving and faithful. God's loving, faithful freedom and our loving, faithful freedom will write beautiful stories.

People who are in love seem to experience the world differently from the way that others experience it. Being in love colors every aspect of their life. Some philosophers talk about knowledge by connaturality, and I think that a loving permanent commitment can provide that kind of knowledge. Connatural knowledge seems to go beyond concepts, ideas and images and is a knowledge achieved by a feeling or sympathy the knower has for the object known. A farmer can have connatural knowledge of the weather. An athlete can have connatural knowledge of the way to play a game. I like a story about Babe Ruth that I think illustrates connatural knowledge. The Yankees were studying the opposing pitcher and trying to determine what type of pitches he was throwing. They were trying to determine whether he was throwing curves or change-ups or fast balls. Babe Ruth came to bat and hit a home run. As he returned to the dugout after running the bases his teammates asked him about the pitch he had hit: "What did it look like, Babe?" Ruth replied, "It looked good."

Through a loving, permanent commitment, a person can have a connatural knowledge of another person. The experience of loving enables the person to see what previously was missed or to see more deeply what previously was seen only superficially. I will not know a person as deeply as I can until I love that person. Love takes blindfolds off the eyes of the lover.

In trying to shed light on self-donation, Father Haughey appeals to the self-donation that characterizes the Blessed Trinity. Each divine person is uniquely who he is by reason of his self-donation to the other two persons. Haughey writes beautifully about the Father's self-donation to the Son:

> "The Father's commitment to his Son, furthermore, included the unconditional intention that all subsequent existents were to come into being through his Son. All of creation was to be shaped by his own Son's purposes, subject to his dominion, and destined finally for his glory. Anthropomorphically speaking, we might say that the entire future of the universe was shaped by the Father's act of self-donation. It is as if the Father were saying 'Henceforth and forever I will make no choices absolutely or by reason of my sovereignty. My Son will shape the not yet and the created reality which He shapes will be forever filial in my eyes.' The Father's commitment specifies how the future will be configured without at the same time predetermining it." (p. 94)

God the Father has placed the future in his Son's hands. Because of love the Father has taken a chance on us. When you love someone you take a chance. The Father has invited us to make our lives love stories through our free choices. We can either accept the Father's self-donation to us through his Son and live our lives according to God's will, or we can reject the Father's self-donation through his Son and turn ourselves away from God. We have free choice, and God is never going to force us to accept his love. God has total respect for our freedom. When you love, you take a chance on the beloved. The Father has taken a chance on us and will never withdraw his commitment. How our stories turn out depends on us and on how we respond to the gift of God's love for us.

Questions

1. What is your most important life commitment? Why? What other life commitments have you made?

2. Are life commitments more difficult to make today? Why?

3. What commitment has God made to us?

4. How do life commitments nourish and foster freedom?

5. What do you think of marriage annulments?

6. What is the relation between our life commitments and our stories and spiritualities?

Now faith is the assurance of things hoped for, the conviction of things not seen.
Indeed, by faith our ancestors received approval.
By faith we understand that the worlds were prepared by the word of God, so that what is seen was made from things that are not visible.

—HEBREWS 11:1-3

Chapter VII

HOW DRAMA CAN
ENRICH OUR STORIES

ARTISTIC MASTERPIECES can be a great blessing in our lives, not only because they give us pleasure but because they can illuminate the human mystery and, at least indirectly, illuminate the mystery of God. By the experience of and serious reflection on painting or sculpture or music or literature—any of the arts—we can grow as persons and enrich our stories.

I love the theater and I find that even when I disagree with the vision of a playwright, the vision of human existence dramatized on the stage provokes me to deeper reflection on my own story. Three of the great twentieth century playwrights are Edward Albee, Harold Pinter and Tennessee Williams. I cannot completely embrace the philosophical vision of any of these authors and yet I am very grateful to each for the illumination and insights they have given me. Viewing their plays or even reading about them can remind us of the indispensable role a talented and insightful playwright has in a society. More than 2000 years ago the philosopher Plato warned the poets that if they got the people too emotionally upset, they would be banished from the state. Plato, though his philosophy of art may be the weakest part of his philosophical vision, saw one thing clearly: he saw what a powerful influence the artist can have on an audience.

Albee, Pinter and Williams are exceptionally skilled dramatists whose plays can touch people very deeply. They are so skilled in their writing that when their plays are revived new directors and new performers may see meanings in them that were either missed or not sufficiently emphasized when the plays were first produced.

I have never seen Albee's *Who's Afraid of Virginia Wolf* on stage but I can vividly recall the first time I saw it on the screen. Albee's script is a frightening vision of contemporary marriage. Throughout the play, the husband goes after the wife and tries to exercise emotional and psychological control over her and the wife makes the same effort in relation to the husband. There is no letup in the psychological and emotional violence that each does to the other. Finally in the last moments of the play they seem to reach an agreement to approach one another and their problems honestly. There is some glimmer of hope for the relationship.

What does such a grim view of human relationships have to offer? It can seem so bleak. Still Albee does have powerful insights into the damage that one person can do to another through deception and lack of love. By showing so vividly and brilliantly the dark side of human nature, Albee provides marvelous material to move us to reflect on our own relationships.

Edward Albee's view of reality is bleak but what he sees he sees so deeply that even though I disagree with him I find his plays a real gift. He sees one dimension of human nature very clearly and presents it powerfully. Some of us might like to forget about the evil in human nature or overlook it but playwrights like Albee won't allow us. Viewing his plays can be painful but redemptive. We live by stories, even stories that might not tell us the whole truth.

The plot of Albee's *A Delicate Balance* involves a long-married man and woman, Tobias and Agnes. As the play opens Agnes is considering the possibility that someday she might lose her mind. That is one balance to which the title of the play refers. Agnes' sister, Claire, who has a serious drinking problem, lives with them, and their daughter, Julia, calls to say that she is going to come home after the collapse of her fourth marriage. Edna and Harry, the best friends of Tobias and Agnes, come to visit and announce their plan to stay. They have been stricken by an unnamed terror, and they look to their friends for shelter and help.

What is the unnamed terror? Should Tobias and Agnes feel some obligation to help? Why does Claire have the drinking problem? Is it related to the fact that for a short time she had a love affair with her sister's husband? And why does Julia have such difficulty with a marriage commitment?

I suppose what I like most about *A Delicate Balance* is the way that Albee relentlessly tries to show the truth about an extremely dysfunctional family. He never lets up; and he will not allow us, the audience, to settle for some simple solution. Though I am not sure, I think that the terror which the friends of Tobias and Agnes experience is the fear that nothing is significant, that nothing matters, and that fear becomes too much for them. What Albee has dramatized for us is a group of people who have no center, no purpose other than getting through each day. Their only purpose seems to be to survive. Those of us who think that there is an ultimate purpose, who believe that our faith is the center of our lives, can still be shaken by Albee's drama. In showing the failures in interpersonal relationships among the characters in the play, Albee forces us to look at our own faults and failures.

The one explicitly religious play that Albee wrote is *Tiny Alice*. What Albee is exploring in *Tiny Alice* is the relationship between belief or unbelief in God and the perception of the rest of reality. The main character, Brother Julian, is sent by a cardinal to collect a huge donation from a benefactor named Alice. When the brother arrives at Alice's mansion, he discovers in her living room a miniature model of the mansion. When Alice first appears, she seems to be an unattractive elderly woman but quickly Julian discovers that she is wearing a mask and that in fact she is a young attractive woman. With this disguise the problem of discerning what is real and what is only apparent is introduced. In terms of the entire play this is one of the key themes. Is God real or only apparent? Do believers believe in a real God or only in an idea of God?

As the play develops we learn that Brother Julian has spent six years in an asylum after having something like a mental breakdown. His breakdown is related to his faith or a least to his temporary loss of the faith that he had. He says that he put himself into the asylum because he could not reconcile himself to the chasm between the nature of God and the use to which men put God. Insisting that this is not a question of semantics, Julian says that men create a false God in their own image because it makes life easier for them. Julian insists that his faith and his sanity are one.

Later in the play Julian notices that there is a fire on the second floor of the miniature house and the other characters become very upset and rush upstairs to put out a fire on the second floor of the mansion. We begin to realize that the miniature model is in some way real and the mansion is in some way an imitation. Albee is forcing us to ask what is real and what is imitation. To add to the mystery, in the living room of the miniature house there is a smaller miniature model of the miniature house, and we wonder if the houses aren't something like a Chinese box with a seemingly never ending succession of smaller houses. Is each smaller house more real than that which it models? Is the real God to be found beyond all the images and theologies that people have created and constructed? This I think is what preoccupies Albee in *Tiny Alice*.

The title of the play is related to Julian's marriage to the Alice who seems to own the mansion. After the ceremony Julian is informed that he is not married to the woman who he thought he married but rather is married to Tiny Alice who presumably inhabits one of the smaller miniature houses, probably the smallest. At this point in the play it seems clear that Tiny Alice is a stand-in for God or perhaps for the non-existence of God.

I think that Albee's play is saying either that there is no God beyond all of our human images of God or that the God who is beyond all our human images can only be reached through a mystical experience, almost through a dark night of the soul. At the end of the play Julian is in a position that the stage directions say should appear like a crucifixion. Of course this image might support either interpretation. Whichever interpretation is correct, and perhaps Albee is deliberately leaving the interpretation to the audience, *Tiny Alice* is a fascinating play.

I have read or seen on stage or in film several Tennessee

Williams plays: *A Streetcar Name Desire, The Rose Tatoo, A Cat on a Hot Tin Roof* and *The Night of the Iguana*. Williams and Eugene O'Neill are often judged to be America's greatest playwrights. Both wrote plays that could break hearts. Both artists saw with great clarity the pain and suffering that human beings experience, and both were very sensitive to the failures of human relationships.

Williams once said that he always had the feeling that he was black. He may have been alluding to his experience of being an outsider in our society, someone not accepted in the mainstream. Perhaps his being gay contributed to that feeling.

Williams' plays seem to dwell on the sordid and the perverse, but they also seem to be a search for purity. Frequent themes in Williams' writings are the fear of loneliness, the experience of loss and death, the search for a lost ideal such as youth and purity. Certainly one of his themes is the opposition between honesty and mendacity. He was repelled by the dog-eat-dog atmosphere he found in the contemporary world. The plot of Williams' *The Night of the Iguana* deals with a defrocked Anglican priest who is conducting tours in Mexico. He spends a long night in conversation with a spinster lady who is caring for her aged dying grandfather, a poet who is trying to finish his master work. Some of Williams' dialogue seems almost poetic.

In the third act the priest, Shannon, and the spinster, Hannah, are having a lengthy conversation. Hannah tells Shannon that she knows what his problem is:

> Hannah: The oldest one in the world—the need to believe in something or in someone—almost anyone—almost anything...something.

Shannon: Your voice sounds hopeless about it.

Hannah: No, I'm not hopeless about it. In fact, I've discovered something to believe in.

Shannon: Something like...God?

Hannah: No.

Shannon: What?

Hannah: Broken gates between people so they can reach each other, even if it's just for one night only.

Shannon: One night stands, huh?

Hannah: One night...communication between them on a veranda outside their...separate cubicles, Mr. Shannon.

Shannon: You don't mean physically, do you?

Hannah: No.

Shannon: I didn't think so. Then what?

Hannah: A little understanding exchanged between them, a wanting to help each other through nights like these.

This may seem like a minimal faith, but it is seeing compassionately into the human mystery and into the experience of loneliness. Williams did not incorporate into his plays a profound Christian faith, but he did incorporate a deep sensitivity to people's loneliness and suffering, and he expressed these human experiences in absolutely beautiful language.

God: Offstage or Onstage?

Perhaps even more "godless" than the world of Albee, and Williams is the world depicted by atheistic existentialist philosopher, Jean-Paul Sartre, in his play *No Exit*. In trying to teach Sartre to undergraduate students I find that he contrasts dramatically with personalist philosophers such as the Roman Catholic existentialist, Gabriel

Marcel. In his vision of human existence, Sartre puts enormous emphasis on human freedom. I have come to think of Sartre as the opposite of Sigmund Freud. Sartre says that we are completely free, that almost nothing hinders or curbs our freedom in any way; Freud says that we have no freedom. Influenced by mechanistic philosophers, Freud, for all his brilliance, missed the mystery of freedom. Some commentators have noted that Sartre, whose philosophy is atheistic, seems to have given divine freedom to people.

What is really sad about Sartre's view of freedom, however, is that it makes no room for God. Sartre thought that if God existed then we could not be free. If there was a God then that God would control our lives. Insisting that humans are free, Sartre concluded that there cannot be a God. Also sad is Sartre's view of love. Sartre believed that all apparent love relationships tended and indeed were doomed to be either sadistic or masochistic. In other words, either the lover controlled the beloved and this would be sadistic because the lover would be trying to take away the beloved's freedom, or the lover surrendered his or her freedom to the beloved and this would be masochistic. Either way a permanent love relationship in which both people remain free is impossible.

Marcel's view of love is dramatically different from Sartre's. Marcel says that it is through interpersonal love that we come to grow as persons and that opening ourselves to God does not make us unfree but rather makes us more free. Loving and being loved leads us to a deeper and deeper freedom.

In Sartre's play *No Exit* there is no escape from freedom, but freedom appears as a kind of curse. Elsewhere Sartre said that we were condemned to be free. Discussing the play with my students reminded me that we are not condemned to be free but rather that we are called to be free, that as we grow in our relationships with other human persons and with God we are growing in freedom. In trying to free people we are acting like God.

Questions

1. What dramas, read or seen, have influenced you? Which influenced you the most and why?
2. Do you agree or disagree with the vision of life expressed in plays by Albee, Pinter, and Williams? How?

*Yet whatever gains I had, these I have come to regard as loss
because of Christ.*

*More than that, I regard everything as loss because of the
surpassing value of knowing Christ Jesus my Lord. For his
sake I have suffered the loss of all things, and I regard them
as rubbish, in order that I may gain Christ*

*and be found in him, not having a righteousness of my own
that comes from the law, but one that comes through faith in
Christ, the righteousness from God based on faith.*

*I want to know Christ and the power of his resurrection and
the sharing of his sufferings by becoming like him in his
death,*

if somehow I may attain the resurrection from the dead.

*Not that I have already obtained this or have already reached
the goal; but I press on to make it my own, because Christ
Jesus has made me his own.*

*Beloved, I do not consider that I have made it my own; but
this one thing I do: forgetting what lies behind and straining
forward to what lies ahead.*

*I press on toward the goal for the prize of the heavenly call of
God in Christ Jesus.*

—PHILIPPIANS 3:7-14

Chapter VIII

CONCLUSION

HUMAN LIVING is an adventure. Every person writes his or her story through free choices. We are neither mechanically-operated robots nor blindly-reacting animals. We are persons and through our intelligence and freedom we shape our lives meaningfully. We are the authors of our stories. But no one writes alone. We are co-authors. God has made a commitment to us. We have been offered a gift. Jesus Christ is God's gift to us. Whether we accept or reject God's gift will determine the ultimate meaning of our stories. May all of us write love stories!

Published by Resurrection Press

A Rachel Rosary *Larry Kupferman*	$3.95
Catholic Is Wonderful *Mitch Finley*	$4.95
Common Bushes *Kieran Kay*	$8.95
Christian Marriage *John & Therese Boucher*	$3.95
Come, Celebrate Jesus! *Francis X. Gaeta*	$4.95
From Holy Hour to Happy Hour *Francis X. Gaeta*	$7.95
Glory to Glory *Francis Clare, SSND*	$9.95
Healing through the Mass *Robert DeGrandis, SSJ*	$7.95
Healing the Wounds of Emotional Abuse *Nancy Benvenga*	$6.95
Healing Your Grief *Ruthann Williams, OP*	$7.95
Living Each Day by the Power of Faith *Barbara Ryan*	$8.95
Inwords *Mary Kraemer, OSF*	$4.50
The Healing of the Religious Life *Faricy/Blackborow*	$6.95
The Joy of Being a Catechist *Gloria Durka*	$4.50
The Joy of Being a Eucharistic Minister *Mitch Finley*	$4.95
Transformed by Love *Margaret Magdalen, CSMV*	$5.95
RVC Liturgical Series: The Liturgy of the Hours	$3.95
The Lector's Ministry	$3.95
Behold the Man *Judy Marley, SFO*	$4.50
Lights in the Darkness *Ave Clark, O.P.*	$8.95
Loving Yourself for God's Sake *Adolfo Quezada*	$5.95
Practicing the Prayer of Presence *van Kaam/Muto*	$7.95
5-Minute Miracles *Linda Schubert*	$3.95
Nothing but Love *Robert Lauder*	$3.95
Healthy and Holy under Stress *van Kaam/Muto*	$3.95
Season of New Beginnings *Mitch Finley*	$4.50
Season of Promises *Mitch Finley*	$4.50
Soup Pot *Ethel Pochocki*	$8.95
Stay with Us *John Mullin, SJ*	$3.95
Surprising Mary *Mitch Finley*	$7.95
What He Did for Love *Francis X. Gaeta*	$4.95

For a free catalog call 1-800-892-6657